# GAO
### Accountability * Integrity * Reliability
# Highlights

Highlights of GAO-12-563T, a testimony before the Subcommittee on Strategic Forces, Committee on Armed Services, U.S. Senate

## SPACE ACQUISITIONS

## DOD Faces Challenges in Fully Realizing Benefits of Satellite Acquisition Improvements

I0426411

## Why GAO Did This Study

Each year, the DOD spends billions on large space acquisition programs, which have in the past experienced cost and schedule overruns and increased technical risk. At present, though, the worst of these problems may be over, and programs long troubled are finally being launched. Challenges persist, but they are less significant than they were. With today's fiscal constraints, however, DOD must find ways to keep its new major space acquisitions on track, as operating in space is expensive and DOD is still replenishing legacy programs like missile warning, protected communications, and environmental monitoring. Significant barriers exist to ensuring such investments are optimized.

To address the progress DOD has made this year, this testimony will focus on (1) the current status of space system acquisitions; (2) results of GAO's space-related reviews this past year; (3) actions taken to address DOD space acquisition problems; and (4) remaining challenges that stand in the way of DOD fully realizing the benefits of satellite acquisition improvements. This testimony is based on previously issued GAO products as well as analysis of DOD funding estimates.

GAO does not make recommendations in this testimony. However, in previous reports GAO has generally recommended that DOD adopt best practices for developing space systems such as separating technology development from product development. DOD is in the process of implementing such practices.

View GAO-12-563T. For more information, contact Cristina Chaplain at (202) 512-4841 or chaplainc@gao.gov.

## What GAO Found

Last year, GAO testified that though acquisition problems still existed in many space programs, the Department of Defense (DOD) was beginning to launch satellites that had long been lagging behind schedule and it had taken positive actions to instill better practices and more focused leadership for space. Progress has continued. Over the past year, DOD launched the first Navy Mobile User Objective System (MUOS) satellite; the first, after a nine-year delay, of six Space Based Infrared System (SBIRS) geosynchronous earth orbit (GEO) satellites; and the first Advanced Extremely High Frequency (AEHF) satellite—all of which will bring important capability to the warfighter. While these launches represent solid progress, there have also been some drawbacks. For instance, the second Global Positioning System (GPS) IIF satellite experienced technical problems that could shorten its operational lifetime. The cost of the first two GPS III satellites is at least 18 percent higher than first estimated, up to $1.6 billion today. A 1-year delay is expected by SBIRS program officials on production of the 3rd and 4th GEO satellites along with a $438 million cost overrun. And, a termination of the Defense Weather Satellite System (DWSS) may result in a capability gap. Moreover, even though problems have been overcome, DOD must still contend with the effects of its previous difficulties on its investment portfolio.

Recent GAO reviews highlight other difficulties facing DOD space programs. GAO's review of a new acquisition strategy for the Evolved Expendable Launch Vehicle program, for instance, identified a need for more knowledge about the industrial base as well as cost and pricing in order to optimize a sizable investment in launch vehicles. GAO's review of parts quality problems in major DOD, Missile Defense Agency, and National Aeronautics and Space Administration (NASA) programs illustrated that acquisition reforms need to be buttressed with closer attention to the quality of piece parts as issues have vexed most major programs. GAO, however, credited the agencies with instituting collaborative efforts to address supplier quality.

Though it still faces an array of challenges, DOD continues to work to ensure its space programs are more executable and produce a better return on investment. For example, DOD intends to follow incremental or evolutionary acquisition processes and it has acted to streamline management and oversight of the national security space enterprise. The agency has taken steps toward reforming the defense acquisition system to help its programs to meet planned cost and schedule objectives. Because DOD intends to address the root causes of problems, it will take time to determine if these actions are successful or need further actions on how best to lead, organize, and support space activities.

Moreover, there are significant barriers to ensuring investments are optimized. These include fragmented leadership, the rising cost of launch, uncertainty about the future for technology advancements, and disconnects between the fielding of satellites with user equipment and ground systems needed to take advantage of expensive new capabilities. Addressing all of these challenges are needed to maintain space superiority in an era of fiscal austerity, but their resolution also requires the participation and cooperation of all the military services, the intelligence community, and agencies such as NASA and the National Oceanic and Atmospheric Administration.

_____ **United States Government Accountability Office**

Chairman Nelson, Ranking Member Sessions, and Members of the Subcommittee:

I am pleased to be here today to discuss the Department of Defense's (DOD) space acquisitions. Each year, billions of dollars are spent by DOD to acquire space-based capabilities that support military and other government operations—such as intelligence, reconnaissance and surveillance, and homeland security— and to enable transformation of the way DOD collects and disseminates information. The worst of DOD's space acquisition problems may be behind the department, as programs long plagued by serious cost and schedule overruns are finally being launched. Though acquisition challenges persist, they are not as widespread and significant as they were several years ago, and to its credit, DOD has taken an array of actions to reduce risks. The challenge DOD now faces is how best to keep its major space systems acquisitions on track in light of fiscal constraints. Operating in space is expensive and DOD is still in the process of replenishing legacy capabilities, such as missile warning, protected communications, and environmental monitoring. While upgrading existing satellite constellations amid declining budgets is a daunting challenge, there are significant barriers to ensuring investments are optimized, including fragmented leadership, the rising cost of launch, uncertainty about the future for technology advancements, and disconnects between the fielding of satellites with user equipment and ground systems needed to take advantage of expensive new capabilities. In addition to discussing the progress DOD has made this year, my testimony will focus on these challenges as they stand in the way of DOD fully realizing the benefits of satellite acquisition improvements.

The objectives of this testimony are to address (1) the current status of space system acquisitions, (2) the results of GAO's space-related reviews this past year, (3) actions being taken to address DOD space acquisition problems, and (4) remaining challenges. In preparing this testimony, we relied on previous GAO reports on (1) space programs and (2) weapon system acquisition best practices as well as ongoing work on satellite control networks.[1] We also relied on work performed in support of our annual weapons system assessments, and analyzed DOD funding estimates to assess cost increases and investment trends for selected

---

[1] See GAO related reports at the end of this statement.

major space system acquisition programs. We obtained updates on improvement actions from the Office of the Secretary of Defense and Air Force. We also analyzed recent funding estimates for space programs. More information on our scope and methodology is available in the issued reports. The work that supports this statement was performed in accordance with generally accepted government auditing standards. Those standards require that we plan and perform the audit to obtain sufficient, appropriate evidence to provide a reasonable basis for our findings and conclusions based on our audit objectives. We believe that the evidence obtained provides a reasonable basis for our findings and conclusions based on our audit objectives.

## Background

The past decade has been troubling for defense space acquisitions. Despite years of significant investment, most of the DOD large space acquisition programs collectively experienced billions of dollars in cost increases, stretched schedules, and increased technical risks. Significant schedule delays of as much as 9 years have resulted in potential capability gaps in missile warning, military communications, and weather monitoring. Unit costs for one of the most troubled programs, the Space Based Infrared System (SBIRS), for instance, have climbed about 231 percent to over $3 billion per satellite. Moreover, the first satellite was launched about 9 years later than predicted. Similarly, by the end of fiscal year 2010, the U.S. government had spent 16 years and over $5 billion to develop the National Polar-orbiting Operational Environmental Satellite System (NPOESS), but had not launched a single satellite. In February 2010, citing the program's cost overruns, schedule delays, and management problems, the White House announced that the NPOESS tri-agency structure would be eliminated and the program would be restructured by splitting procurements and responsibilities. Other programs, such as the Transformational Satellite Communications System, were canceled several years earlier because they were found to be too highly ambitious and not affordable at a time when the DOD was struggling to address critical acquisition problems elsewhere in the space portfolio.

# The Current Status of Space System Acquisitions

In 2011, we testified that though problems still existed on many programs, DOD was beginning to make progress by finally launching satellites that had been lagging behind schedule.[2] These included the Missile Defense Agency's (MDA) Space Tracking and Surveillance System (STSS), the Air Force's first Global Positioning System (GPS) IIF satellite and the first Advanced Extremely High Frequency (AEHF) satellite although AEHF had not yet reached its final planned orbit at the time we testified because of an anomaly with the satellite's propulsion system. At the same time, however, several programs still in development were at risk of cost and schedule growth, such as the Joint Space Operations Center Mission System (JMS).

Progress has continued since we testified last year. For instance:

- DOD launched the second GPS IIF satellite in July 2011, and the third is scheduled to launch in September 2012.
- DOD launched the first of the Navy's Mobile User Objective System (MUOS) satellites in February 2012, and the second is scheduled for launch in July 2013.
- The first of six SBIRS geosynchronous earth orbit (GEO) satellites successfully launched in May 2011, after a roughly 9 year delay.[3] The second SBIRS satellite is planned for delivery in spring 2012 and may launch late this year or early 2013.
- The Evolved Expendable Launch Vehicle (EELV) program continues to successfully launch DOD and National Aeronautics and Space Administration (NASA) satellites, and is planning 11 launches in 2012.
- The first AEHF satellite reached its intended orbit after having experienced propulsion trouble after launch. The second AEHF satellite is scheduled to launch in April 2012.

While these launches represent solid progress, there have been some drawbacks to the programs that have launched their first satellites. For instance, the second GPS IIF satellite experienced technical problems that could possibly shorten the satellite's operational lifetime. Also, though a MUOS satellite has been launched, the DOD estimates that over 90 percent of the first satellite's on-orbit capabilities will likely be initially

---

[2] GAO, *Space Acquisitions: DOD Delivering New Generations of Satellites, but Space System Acquisition Challenges Remain*, GAO-11-590T (Washington, D.C.: May 11, 2011).

[3] Two highly elliptical orbit sensors have already been launched.

underutilized because of delays in development of the compatible Joint Tactical Radio System (JTRS) terminals.

Moreover, other acquisition programs are experiencing cost and schedule growth, though not to the extent yet as those experienced in the last decades. For instance,

- The GPS III program is currently experiencing cost growth and the contractor is behind schedule. In November 2011, the contractor's estimated cost at completion for the development and production of the first two satellites was over $1.4 billion or 18 percent greater than originally estimated; the program office estimated the cost to be about $1.6 billion. The GPS III program has cited multiple reasons for the projected cost increases including reductions in the program's production rate; test equipment delays; and inefficiencies in the development of both the navigation and communication payload and satellite bus. The contractor is also behind in completing some tasks on schedule, but the program does not expect these delays to affect the launch of the first satellite.
- Though the first SBIRS satellite has launched, and the second is close to delivery, program officials are predicting a 1-year delay on production of the 3rd and 4th GEO satellites due in part to technical challenges, parts obsolescence and test failures. Along with the production delay, program officials are predicting a $438 million cost overrun for the 3rd and 4th GEO satellites.
- The Defense Weather Satellite System (DWSS), which was the Air Force's follow-on to the restructured NPOESS, was terminated in fiscal year 2012. The restructuring of NPOESS and the subsequent cancellation of DWSS have resulted in a potential capability gap for weather and environmental monitoring.

Table 1 describes the status of the space programs we have been tracking in more detail.

## Table 1: Status of Major Space Acquisition Efforts

### Programs still susceptible to cost and schedule overruns

| | |
|---|---|
| **GPS IIF**<br>(positioning, navigation, and timing) | The second Global Positioning System (GPS) IIF satellite, designed to upgrade timing and navigation accuracy and add a new signal for civilian use, launched on July 16, 2011, and the third is expected to launch in September of 2012. Approximately one month after they were enabled, the second IIF satellite's Cesium clock—one of three atomic frequency standard clocks onboard that provide GPS accuracy through redundancy—failed. An investigation identified design and manufacturing issues, and the GPS Directorate is exploring options, including replacing the Cesium clocks already installed on the remaining IIF satellites, 3 through 7. The cost and schedule impacts are as yet undetermined. According to the GPS directorate, the cost of the GPS IIF program, as of April 2011, was at $2.6 billion—more than triple the original cost estimate of $729 million. The IIF satellites' development challenges were mostly responsible for the 4 1/2-year delay in the launch of the first GPS IIF satellite to May 2010. |
| **AEHF**<br>(communications) | On August 14, 2010, the Air Force launched the first of six planned Advanced Extremely High Frequency (AEHF) satellites (AEHF-1) to replenish the existing Milstar system with increased strategic and tactical capabilities for warfighters. Employing a novel combination of chemical and electric propulsion in a two-phase orbit raising procedure, AEHF-1 was expected to reach its operational orbit in about three months. However, an anomaly with one of the spacecraft's three propulsion systems delayed the arrival on orbit by about 13 months. The anomaly was detected when the spacecraft's Liquid Apogee Engine (LAE)—a bi-propellant system designed to provide the thrust for the spacecraft's initial orbit transfer maneuvers—faltered and was declared unusable. No longer able to use the more powerful LAE for the first phase of orbit raising as intended, the program office in conjunction with the contractor and user community, decided to achieve the intended orbit using AEHF-1's two remaining, less powerful propulsion systems. The alternate propulsion was engaged and the spacecraft's rate of ascent was calculated to conserve fuel and maintain its original 14-year operational life expectancy. AEHF-1 reached its intended orbit in late October 2011, and began undergoing what is expected to be about 100 days of testing. The problem with AEHF-1 was not identified on either AEHF-2, which has been delivered and is on schedule for an April 27, 2012 launch, or AEHF-3, which is currently in storage and expected to launch in the fall of 2013. The fourth satellite is under contract and scheduled to be available for launch in 2017. Plans to procure the last two AEHF satellites—tentatively expected to be available for launch in 2018 and 2019— were announced following the 2009 cancellation of the Transformational Satellite Communications System—the planned follow-on to AEHF. |
| **MUOS**<br>(communications) | The first Mobile User Objective System (MUOS) communications satellite was launched on February 24, 2012, and is expected to begin on-orbit operations in May 2012—26 months later than planned at development start. While the delivery of the MUOS satellite's ultra-high frequency (UHF) communication capabilities is predicted to help address the potential capability gap caused by the unexpected failure of two legacy satellites, there is a risk the satellite's on-orbit capabilities will initially be significantly underutilized. Over 90 percent of MUOS's planned capability—including increases in the amount of data that can be transmitted and the ability to transmit both voice and data—is enabled by compatible Joint Tactical Radio System (JTRS) terminals and by a new waveform. Operational testing of the JTRS terminals has been delayed until February 2014, leading the government to form an independent review team to assess potential options for completing development of the MUOS waveform. Following a 2009 Navy-initiated review, the program developed new cost and schedule baselines. However, the MUOS acquisition program baseline has been under revision since December 2009, and has not yet been approved. |

| | |
|---|---|
| **GPS III**<br>(positioning, navigation, and timing) | GPS is a constellation of multiple generations of GPS satellites that provide global position, navigation and timing capability to both military and civil users worldwide. In 2008 the GPS directorate established a program to develop the next generation of GPS satellites named GPS III. GPS III satellites are designed to have the capabilities found on GPS IIF satellites plus increases in jam resistance, accuracy, and design life; a new civil signal compatible with the European Galileo system; and a satellite bus capable of supporting future satellite capability additions. The GPS III program is to use an acquisition strategy designed to reduce risk and to avoid or correct problems that plagued the GPS IIF program and caused a more than 4 year delay in the launch of the first IIF satellite. The GPS III program plans to maintain stable requirements; have rigorous contractor oversight; and employ a structured systems engineering approach which includes features such as trade studies, advanced component development and prototype, and incremental delivery of mature technologies. One of the program's risk reduction efforts includes research on dual launch initiatives to support two satellites launching on one launch vehicle. The GPS program office attributes current cost growth issues to reductions in the program's production rate, test equipment delays, and inefficiencies in the development of both the navigation and communication payload and satellite bus. The program office and contractor have estimated the cost to complete the development and production of the first two GPS III satellites at $1.6 billion and $1.4 billion respectively, which is 18 percent or more than originally estimated. The first GPS III satellite is expected to be ready for launch in May of 2014. |

## Development initiatives getting under way

| | |
|---|---|
| **JMS**<br>(space situational awareness) | Space Situational Awareness (SSA)—the knowledge and characterization of space objects and the environment on which space operations depend—is increasingly important to the protection of U.S. space forces from space weather effects, space debris, and attack. The Joint Space Operations Center Mission System (JMS) program is a key component of SSA and one of two major upcoming acquisition efforts (the other is Space Fence) expected to fill the growing need to replace SSA capability from fragmented legacy systems and to provide new, advanced SSA capability. The JMS program is designed to replace the Space Defense Operations Center (SPADOC) currently in use but nearing the end of its operational lifetime, and provide mission services to support and enable the command and control of space forces. In early 2011, the Office of the Under Secretary of Defense for Acquisition, Technology and Logistics commissioned an independent program assessment of the JMS program which, at that time, had plans to use immature technologies and to deliver key capabilities in a single, large increment, versus smaller and more manageable increments. In May 2011, in response to concerns raised by the assessment, the Air Force announced the transfer of JMS to the management group responsible for most of the service's space-related acquisition and the implementation of a new tailored incremental information technology acquisition approach. According to officials at the new JMS program office, the revised approach is modeled on tenets from DOD's 2007 Defense Acquisition Transformation Report to Congress and includes plans to maximize the use of commercial-off-the-shelf and government-off-the-shelf solutions, to leverage investment in existing government prototypes and industry applications, and to utilize personnel from other services or federal labs who have expertise in relevant technologies and systems. |

| | |
|---|---|
| **Space Fence**<br>(space situational awareness) | Space Fence is being designed as a system of geographically dispersed ground-based radars. It is intended to replace and expand coverage currently provided by the aging Space Surveillance System by using higher radio frequencies that will allow it to detect and track smaller Earth-orbiting objects. Like JMS, Space Fence is a key program to help meet the nation's SSA mission and represents the current largest investment in SSA at an estimated cost of about $3 billion to complete. Space Fence program officials have stated that Space Fence will be one of the largest phased array radars ever built. The size of the radar is expected to provide significant power for the transmission and reception of data but may also pose increased risk related to the affordable integration of technology components. To mitigate this risk, the Space Fence acquisition strategy includes maintaining competition through technology development and having two firms under contract doing parallel prototype development. This process allows program officials to evaluate contractor's designs and associated costs while moving Space Fence's four critical technologies and backup technologies toward maturity, before the program enters system development which is scheduled for later this year with the award of a single contract. Though earlier plans called for the first Space Fence site to achieve initial operational capability in 2015, estimates show that at current funding levels, this capability will not occur before 2017. |
| **PTSS**<br>(ballistic missile defense) | The Precision Tracking Space System (PTSS) is being developed as an operational component of the Missile Defense Agency's (MDA) Ballistic Missile Defense System and, according to MDA, delays in fielding a PTSS constellation in fiscal year 2018 would significantly affect the implementation of the Phased Adaptive Approach (PAA) to defend Europe and the United States against regional ballistic missile attacks. We have on-going MDA work and have initial concerns regarding schedule optimism, concurrency, and potential cost estimates. We plan to issue a report on the results of our review in April 2012. |
| **SBSS**<br>(space situational awareness) | On February 23, 2011, the Space Based Space Surveillance (SBSS) satellite began full operational duty. The satellite was launched in September 2010, to provide a follow-on capability to the Midcourse Space Experiment / Space Based Visible sensor satellite, which ended its mission in July 2008. According to program and contracting officials, SBSS' 24-hour, all-weather, all-geography capability provides an increase in space situational awareness—the ability to search, detect, and track objects in space—by a factor of three compared to ground based tools. Air Force stated that the timing of the SBSS launch and the magnitude of initial cost estimates for the proposed SBSS follow-on led to the decision not to include funding for this effort in their fiscal year 2012 budget request. In fiscal year 2013 the Air Force plans to initiate acquisition strategy plans for the SBSS follow-on, including preparing for the competitive award of a fixed price contract meeting or exceeding SBSS Block 10 requirements. |

| NPOESS/DWSS/ WSF (climate and weather monitoring) | The National Polar-orbiting Operational Environmental Satellite System (NPOESS) was planned to be a state-of-the-art, environment-monitoring satellite system that would replace two existing polar-orbiting environmental satellite systems—one managed by the Department of Commerce's National Oceanic and Atmospheric Administration (NOAA) and the other by the Department of Defense (DOD)/U.S. Air Force. The NPOESS program was jointly managed by NOAA, DOD/ Air Force, and the National Aeronautics and Space Administration (NASA), and considered critical to the nation's weather forecasting and climate monitoring needs through the year 2026. In February 2010, the White House's Office of Science and Technology Policy restructured the NPOESS program to address continuing cost, schedule, management, and technical challenges. Furthermore, DOD/Air Force and NOAA/NASA were directed to plan and acquire their own replacement satellite systems. The Air Force initiated preliminary efforts on the Defense Weather Satellite System (DWSS) as its next-generation polar-orbiting environmental satellite system with primary earth coverage in the early morning. To reduce development risks and lower acquisition costs, the Air Force planned to leverage the billions of dollars invested in the NPOESS program. Furthermore, to ensure continued coverage, the Air Force had planned to have DWSS satellites available for launch in 2018 and 2021. However, in fiscal year 2012, DWSS was terminated per Congressional direction, and DOD/Air Force budgeted for a new program called the Weather Satellite Follow-on (WSF). Planned program activities include a requirements analysis and an analysis of alternatives. Until the DOD/Air Force transitions from its current Defense Meteorological Satellite Program (DMSP) satellites to a follow-on system, DOD/Air Force plans to continue utilizing the remaining DMSP satellites to meet its weather requirements. |
|---|---|

Source: GAO analysis of DOD data and previous GAO reports.

## Acquisition Challenges Have Reverberating Effects on Investment Portfolio

Even though DOD has finally overcome some technical and production difficulties and begun to launch high risk satellites such as SBIRS and AEHF, the department is still contending with the effects of their significant cost growth on its investment portfolio. Figure 1 compares original cost estimates to current cost estimates for the broader portfolio of major space acquisitions for fiscal years 2011 through 2016.

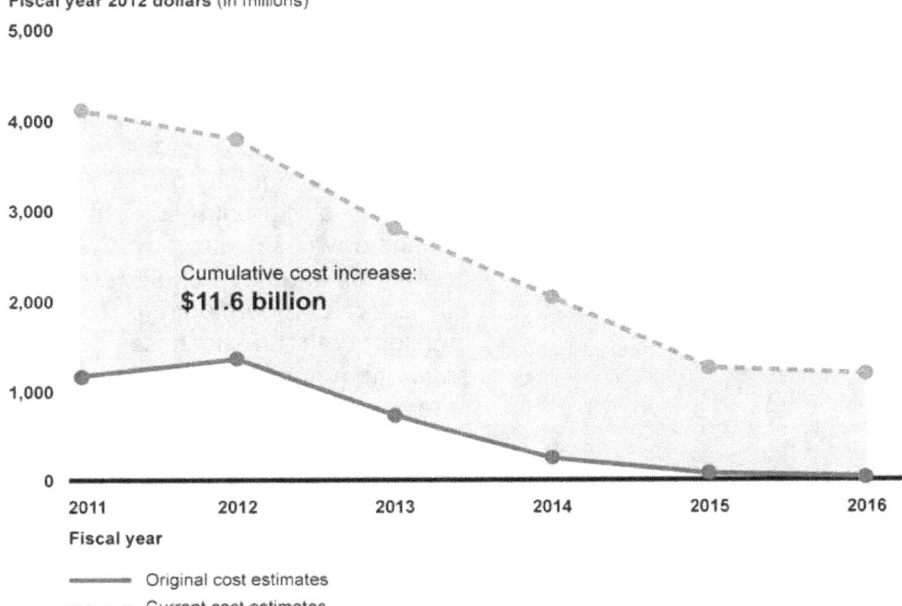

**Figure 1: Comparison between Original Cost Estimates and Current Cost Estimates for Selected Major Space Acquisition Programs for Fiscal Years 2011 through 2016**

Fiscal year 2012 dollars (in millions)

Cumulative cost increase:
**$11.6 billion**

Fiscal year

——— Original cost estimates

– – – Current cost estimates

Source: GAO analysis of DOD data.

Note: Includes Advanced Extremely High Frequency, Global Broadcast System, Global Positioning System II and III, Mobile User Objective System, Space Based Infrared System, and Wideband Global SATCOM. This chart does not include the Evolved Expendable Launch Vehicle, and planned new space acquisition efforts—such as Joint Space Operations Center Mission System, Space Based Space Surveillance Follow-on, the Weather Satellite Follow-on, or Space Fence—for which total cost data were unavailable.

A long-standing problem in DOD space acquisitions is that program and unit costs tend to go up significantly from initial cost estimates, and the gap between original and current estimates shows that DOD has fewer dollars available to invest in new programs or add to existing ones. In fact, estimated costs for the major space acquisition programs have increased by about $11.6 billion—321 percent—from initial estimates for fiscal years 2011 through 2016.[4] It should also be noted that the declining investment in the later years is the result of mature programs that have planned lower out-year funding, cancellation of a major space acquisition

---

[4] Costs adjusted for inflation.

program and several development efforts, and the exclusion of several major space acquisition efforts for which total cost data were unavailable. These include the Space Fence, Space Based Space Surveillance, and the Defense Weather Satellite effort.

## GAO Space-Related Reviews over the Past Year

Over the past year, we have reported on of the need for sound and sufficient information for the new DOD acquisition strategy for the EELV program; parts quality problems in major DOD, MDA, and NASA programs; and greater content and coordination in the space Science and Technology (S&T) strategy. We are also conducting a review of satellite operations and have briefed Defense authorization and appropriations committees on our findings. These reviews, discussed further below, highlight both the successes and challenges that have faced the DOD space community as it has completed or sought to complete problematic legacy efforts and deliver modernized capabilities.

## Evolved Expendable Launch Vehicle Acquisition Strategy

DOD's EELV program serves a vital mission of placing critical national security and civilian satellites into their required orbits. It is also on the brink of major changes. In 2009, the Air Force and the National Reconnaissance Office (NRO) determined that the current approach for acquiring EELV launch vehicles was likely not the best business model and decided that a new acquisition strategy needed to be developed. This strategy favors committing the government to a longer span of purchases and to more certainty in the number of vehicles acquired to help stabilize the industrial base. Such a change is significant as the DOD and the NRO plan to spend about $15 billion to acquire launch services from fiscal year 2013 to 2017 and commercial companies other than the current provider, United Launch Alliance, would like to become launch service providers to the government. We were asked to review and assess whether DOD has the knowledge it needs to develop the new strategy, which has subsequently been released, and to identify issues that could benefit future launch acquisitions.

We found that DOD lacked critical knowledge needed to develop a new acquisition strategy.[5] For example, program officials, recent launch

---

[5] GAO, *Evolved Expendable Launch Vehicle: DOD Needs to Ensure New Acquisition Strategy Is Based on Sufficient Information,* GAO-11-641 (Washington, D.C.: Sep 15, 2011).

studies, and the prime contractor all cited a diminishing launch industrial base as a risk to the mission success of the program, but DOD analysis supporting this condition was minimal. Moreover, under the new acquisition strategy, contracting officials may have difficulty assessing fair and reasonable prices given limited availability of contractor and subcontractor cost or pricing data. Since the United Launch Alliance joint venture formed in 2006, financial and business systems needed to get insight into costs have been lacking. There was also considerable uncertainty about costs associated with mission assurance activities, even though there have been concerns about whether such activities are excessive. Moreover, we found that if the acquisition strategy commits the Air Force and the NRO to buy eight common booster cores per year for a five year period, which was anticipated at the time of our review, DOD may face an oversupply of vehicles. In addition to these findings, we have reported prior concerns about oversight for the EELV program, such as (1) a prior decision to designate the program as in the sustainment phase rather than in the development phase essentially lifted the need for oversight reporting on costs and major changes and (2) the DOD had not updated a life cycle cost estimate for the program despite significant changes being made to it.[6]

Among other actions, we recommended that DOD conduct an independent assessment of the health of the U.S. launch industrial base; reassess the block buy contract length given the additional knowledge DOD is gaining; not waive Federal Acquisition Regulations requirements for contractor and subcontractor certified cost and pricing data as DOD finalizes its strategy; and ensure launch mission assurance activities be sufficient and not excessive. The Congress reinforced these and other GAO recommendations in the National Defense Authorization Act of 2012 by requiring that DOD redesignate the program as a major defense acquisition program (which would require the submission of certain kinds of data annually) and provide to Congressional defense committees a description of how its acquisition strategy will address the recommendations of our EELV report issued in 2011.[7] The Act also requires us to submit an assessment of the information DOD provides,

---

[6] GAO, *Space Acquisitions: Uncertainties in the Evolved Expendable Launch Vehicle Program Pose Management and Oversight Challenges*, GAO-08-1039 (Washington, D.C.: Sep 26, 2008).

[7] Pub. L. No. 112-81, §§ 838 & 839 (2011).

and additional findings or recommendations, as appropriate. The Air Force has taken actions to expand its knowledge about EELV since our 2011 audit work was completed and we look forward to assessing this progress.

## Parts Quality for DOD, MDA, and NASA

Quality is paramount to the success of U.S. space and missile defense programs due to their complexity, the environment they operate in, and the high degree of accuracy and precision needed for their operations. Yet in recent years, many programs have experienced difficulties with quality workmanship and parts. Less visible problems have led to unnecessary repair, scrap, rework, and stoppage; long delays; and millions of dollars in cost growth. In some instances, entire missions have been endangered. As a result, we assessed the extent to which such problems affect related programs, their causes, and what initiatives have been undertaken in response.

We found that parts quality problems had affected all 21 programs we reviewed, in some cases contributing to significant cost overruns and schedule delays associated with electronic versus mechanical parts or materials.[8] We also found that if quality problems were discovered late in the development cycle they had more significant cost and schedule consequences: in one such case, an additional cost of at least $250 million and a 2-year launch delay. We found several causes of these problems: poor workmanship, undocumented and untested manufacturing processes, poor control of those processes and materials and failure to prevent contamination, poor part design, design complexity, and an inattention to manufacturing risks. Ineffective supplier management also resulted in concerns about whether subcontractors and contractors met program requirements.

Recognition of these difficulties has spurred agencies to adopt new policies, but they were still in early stages of implementation at the time of our review. Post-policy programs are not yet mature enough for parts problems to be apparent. To address current and future problems, agencies and industry have begun to collect and share information, develop testing guidance and criteria, manage subcontractors, and

---

[8] GAO, *Space and Missile Defense Acquisitions: Periodic Assessment Needed to Correct Parts Quality Problems in Major Programs,* GAO-11-404 (Washington, D.C.: Jun 24, 2011).

mitigate problems, although their impact has yet to be determined. In any event, significant barriers hinder such efforts, including broader acquisition management problems, workforce gaps, diffuse leadership in the national security space community, the government's decreasing influence on the electronics parts market, and an increase in counterfeited parts. Our reports over the past decade have made recommendations for addressing these broader barriers, such as stabilizing requirements before beginning product development, separating technology development from product development, and strengthening leadership. The DOD is in the process of adopting these recommendations. Because space agencies and the Missile Defense Agency were undertaking additional actions to address parts quality problems and they had recently established a broad range of coordination mechanisms, we recommended that the community undertake periodic assessments of progress being made to address parts quality problems. The agencies generally agreed with our recommendation.

## Space S&T Strategy

The National Defense Authorization Act for Fiscal Year 2010 required DOD and the Director of National Intelligence (DNI) to jointly develop a space S&T strategy and it required us to assess the strategy submitted in April 2011.[9] We reported that a strong foundation in space S&T should help DOD and the intelligence community address the most challenging national security problems, reduce risk in major acquisition programs, maintain technological superiority over adversaries, maintain a healthy industrial base and mitigate vulnerabilities in space systems.[10]

We found that the strategy largely met the requirements of the authorization act, but it was not a rigorous, comprehensive strategic plan. Instead, it embraced the status quo without laying out a path for assuring effective and efficient progress. For instance, the strategy identified goals, but did not prioritize them. The strategy described existing reviews used to assess progress in space S&T but did not identify new metrics or performance measures to be used to assess achievement of the strategy's newly established goals. Nor did the strategy address fundamental challenges facing the S&T community, such as human

---

[9] Pub. L. No. 111-84, § 911(b) (2009).

[10] GAO, *Space Research: Content and Coordination of Space Science and Technology Strategy Need to Be More Robust*, GAO-11-722 (Washington, D.C.: Jul 19, 2011).

capital shortages, growing fiscal pressures, and the difficulty in transitioning space S&T to acquisition programs. We identified some strategic planning best practices such as identifying required human capital and required funding; prioritizing initiatives; and establishing ways to measure progress and processes for revising goals in the future. Additionally, we found that organizations involved in developing the strategy were active in creating its long- and short-term goals, but their participation in other of its aspects was more limited. DOD and DNI officials did not believe they were required to do more than they did, and also did not include other agencies active in space S&T that were not included by law in the strategy. We recommended that DOD enhance its next version of the strategy by developing a detailed implementation plan for achieving goals, addressing funding prioritization and other challenges, and enhancing coordination with other agencies involved in space technology development. DOD concurred with these recommendations.

## DOD Satellite Operations

The Air Force and Navy operate separate satellite control networks within DOD through multiple operations centers, enabling their satellites to perform missions from launch to on-orbit operations and eventually through deactivation. Other federal government agencies, such as the NASA and the National Oceanic and Atmospheric Administration (NOAA), and commercial companies also operate satellites using various networks and operations centers. Combined, these networks assist the nation's communications, missile warning, navigation, meteorological, environmental, and scientific satellites or missions.

DOD has efforts underway to modernize various satellite operations centers using proprietary and interoperable network architectures using standard protocols. For example, since 2006, the Air Force has operated a multi-mission operations center that uses a standard interface and telemetry, tracking, and commanding system which allows expedited transition of research satellites to operational satellites. In addition, in 2000, the Naval Research Laboratory initiated a web-based service concept designed to optimize software code reuse and allow faster delivery of mission capabilities, which could lower mission development costs and facilitate system maintenance. Considering the long-standing need to replace the Air Force's aging and costly satellite control capabilities, and the importance associated with satellite operations, it is important that DOD not miss an opportunity to improve satellite operations and create greater efficiencies by leveraging commercial practices and other satellite networks and associated infrastructure.

In ongoing work, we assessed DOD's satellite operations capabilities, specifically modernization efforts, compare DOD satellite operations concepts with those in other government entities and commercial industry; and, identify practices that could improve DOD satellite operations, consistent with mission requirements. We identified several challenges associated with DOD's modernization efforts. For example, DOD's ability to plan and implement upgrades may be limited by current budget uncertainties and plans to reallocate a portion of DOD's spectrum may affect its satellite operations. In addition, we found indications that the potential for unnecessary overlap and fragmentation still exists within satellite operations and associated infrastructure, including potential duplication of facilities and hardware. For instance, there are multiple, completely separate government satellite control networks that exist that depend on DOD's Air Force satellite control network, including military and civil networks, but none are interoperable. Finally, we have thus far found that although research and development in government satellite operations has led to the use of practices that, according to agency officials, have improved efficiency, there are other commercial practices that could provide further improvements to DOD's satellite network. For example, increased automation of routine satellite telemetry, tracking, and commanding functions could increase satellite operations efficiencies. We expect to issue our report based on this review later this fall.

## Actions Being Taken to Address Space Acquisition Problems

Though our reports over the year indicate there is more room for improvement, DOD continues to work to ensure that its space programs are more executable and produce a better return on investment. Many of the actions it has been taking are intended to address root causes of problems, though it will take time to determine whether these actions are successful and they need to be complemented by decisions on how best to lead, organize, and support space activities.

## Causes of Acquisition Problems

Our past work has identified a number of causes of acquisition problems, but several consistently stand out. At a higher level, DOD has tended to start more weapon programs than is affordable, creating a competition for funding that focuses on advocacy at the expense of realism and sound management. DOD has also tended to start its space programs before it has the assurance that the capabilities it is pursuing can be achieved within available resources and time constraints. There is no way to accurately estimate how long it would take to design, develop, and build a satellite system when critical technologies planned for that system are still in relatively early stages of discovery and invention. Finally, programs have historically attempted to satisfy all requirements in a single step, regardless of the design challenges or the maturity of the technologies necessary to achieve the full capability. DOD's preference to make larger, complex satellites that perform a multitude of missions has stretched technology challenges beyond current capabilities in some cases. Figure 2 illustrates the negative influences that can cause programs to fail.

**Figure 2: Negative Influences that Can Cause Programs to Fail**

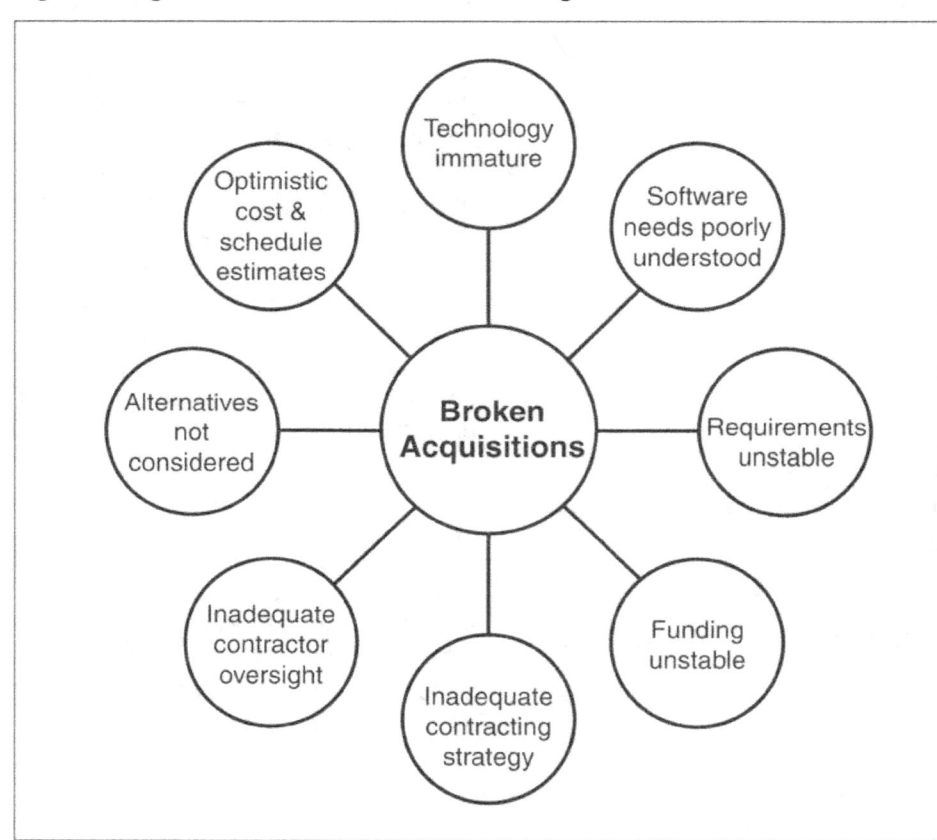

Source: GAO.

Our work has recommended numerous actions that can be taken to address the problems we identified. Generally, we have recommended that DOD separate technology discovery from acquisition, follow an incremental path toward meeting user needs, match resources and requirements at program start, and use quantifiable data and demonstrable knowledge to make decisions to move to next phases. We have also identified practices related to cost estimating, program manager tenure, quality assurance, technology transition, and an array of other aspects of acquisition program management that could benefit space programs.[11] DOD has generally concurred with our recommendations, and, as described below, has undertaken an array of actions to establish a better foundation for acquisition success.

## Actions to Improve Space and Weapon Systems Acquisitions

As we reported last year, DOD has implemented or has been implementing a number of actions to reform how space and weapon systems are acquired, both through its own initiatives as well as those required by statute. Among other actions, DOD intends to follow incremental or evolutionary acquisition processes for space programs versus pursuing significant leaps in capabilities involving technology risk, and has done so with the only new satellite program undertaken by the Air Force in recent years—GPS III and more recently with Joint Space Operations Center Mission System, which supports space situational awareness activities. DOD and the Air Force are also working to streamline management and oversight of the national security space enterprise. For example, all Air Force space system acquisition responsibility has been assigned to the office responsible for all other Air Force acquisition efforts, and options for streamlining the many space committees, boards, and councils is under ongoing review. These and other actions being taken that could improve space system acquisition outcomes, that we have not assessed, are described in table 2.

---

[11] GAO, *Space Acquisitions: DOD Poised to Enhance Space Capabilities but, Persistent Challenges Remain in Developing Space Systems,* GAO-10-447T (Washington, D.C.: March 10, 2010).

**Table 2: Actions Being Taken That Could Benefit Space System Acquisition Outcomes**

| Category | Actions |
|---|---|
| National policy | • In June 2010, the President of the United States issued the new National Space Policy which establishes overarching national policy for the conduct of U.S. space activities. The policy states that the Secretary of Defense and the Director of National Intelligence are responsible for developing, acquiring, and operating space systems and networks to support U.S. national security and enable defense and intelligence operations. The policy helps to clarify the Secretary of Defense's roles and responsibilities for coordinating space system acquisitions that span DOD and federal agencies, such as those for space situational awareness.<br>• In January 2011, the Secretary of Defense and the Director of National Intelligence issued the National Security Space Strategy to build on the National Space Policy and help inform planning, programming, acquisition, operations, and analysis. |
| Acquisitions | • We expressed concern over DOD's tailored national security space acquisition policy—initially issued in 2003—primarily because it did not alter DOD's practice of committing to major investments before knowing what resources will be required to deliver promised capability. Instead, the policy encouraged development of leading-edge technology within product development, that is, at the same time the program manager is designing the system and undertaking other product development activities. In 2009, DOD eliminated the space acquisition policy and moved the acquisition of space systems under DOD's updated acquisition guidance for defense acquisition programs (DOD Instruction 5000.02). In October 2010, the Under Secretary of Defense for Acquisition, Technology and Logistics issued a new space acquisition policy to be incorporated into that instruction that introduces specific management and oversight processes for acquiring major space systems, including retaining the requirement for independent program assessments to be conducted prior to major acquisition milestones. |
| Management and oversight | • In June 2008, the Undersecretary of Defense for Acquisition, Technology and Logistics created the Space and Intelligence Capabilities Office (SIO) to oversee all major DOD space and intelligence related acquisitions, including space-based communications programs, space control activities, space launch ranges, and all related ground systems. The SIO is to develop and recommend policies, investment strategies, and programs that improve, streamline, and strengthen DOD component space and intelligence related system acquisition, organization, technology and development activities.<br>• In May 2009, Air Force leadership signed the Acquisition Improvement Plan which lists five initiatives for improving how the Air Force obtains new capabilities.[a] One of these initiatives relates to establishing clear lines of authority and accountability within acquisition organizations. In August 2010, the Secretary of the Air Force transferred space system acquisition responsibility from the Under Secretary of the Air Force to the Assistant Secretary of the Air Force for Acquisition, thereby assigning all Air Force acquisition responsibility to one office. As part of this realignment, the Program Executive Officer for Space, who previously reported to the Undersecretary of the Air Force, now reports to the Assistant Secretary of the Air Force for Acquisition.<br>• In August 2010, the Secretary of Defense announced the elimination of the Office of the Assistant Secretary of Defense for Networks and Information Integration (ASD/NII) as part of a broader effort to eliminate organizations that perform duplicative functions or that have outlived their purpose.[b] The elimination of this organization may help to reduce the problems associated with the wide range of stakeholders within DOD responsible for overseeing the development of space-based capabilities.<br>• In November 2010, the Deputy Secretary of Defense authorized the disestablishment of the National Security Space Office (NSSO).[c] The elimination of this office may also help to streamline national security space system acquisition management and oversight. Furthermore, the Deputy Secretary of Defense revalidated the Secretary of the Air Force as DOD Executive Agent for Space and directed the creation of a Defense Space Council (DSC)—chaired by the DOD Executive Agent for Space and with representatives from across DOD—to inform, coordinate, and resolve space issues for DOD. According to DOD, the council will be looking at streamlining the many defense and national security space committees, boards, and councils by reviewing more than 15 space-related organizations and making recommendations on their cancellation, consolidation, dissolution, or realignment under the DSC. |

| Category | Actions |
|---|---|
| Program management assistance | • The Space and Missile Systems Center—the Air Force's primary organization responsible for acquiring space systems—resurrected a program management assistance group in 2007 to help mitigate program management, system integration, and program control deficiencies within specific ongoing programs. This group assists and supplements wing commanders and program offices in fixing common problems, raising core competencies, and providing a consistent culture that sweeps across programs. According to the, at the time, Global Positioning System (GPS) Directorate Commander, this group was an integral part of the overall process providing application-oriented training, templates, analyses, and assessments vital to the GPS IIIA baseline review. According to a senior program management assistance group official, the group has provided assistance to other major programs, including GPS ground control segment (OCX), Space Based Infrared System (SBIRS), and Space Based Space Surveillance (SBSS). |
| Workforce | • Another initiative in the Air Force Acquisition Improvement Plan is to revitalize the acquisition workforce by, among other things, increasing the number of authorized positions and providing for additional hiring, examining the proper mix of military and civilian personnel, and establishing training and experience objectives as part of the career paths for each acquisition specialty and increasing the availability of specialized training. As we reported in 2010, the Air Force was continuing efforts to bring space operators and space system acquirers together through the Advanced Space Operations School and the National Security Space Institute. The Air Force anticipated that this higher-level education would be integral to preparing space leaders with the best acquisition know-how. |
| Cost estimating | • The Air Force took actions to strengthen cost estimating. For example, we recommended that the Secretary of the Air Force ensure that cost estimates are updated as major events occur within a program that could have a material impact on cost, and that the roles and responsibilities of the various Air Force cost-estimating organizations be clearly articulated.[d] An Air Force policy directive now requires that cost estimates for major programs be updated annually, and lays out roles and responsibilities for Air Force cost-estimating organizations. Additionally, the Joint Space Cost Council—formed in 2007 with membership across industry and military and civil government agencies—is actively working to improve cost credibility and realism in estimates, budgets, schedules, data, proposals, and program execution. For example, one initiative has developed a standard work breakdown structure that is being vetted through industry and government. |
| Military standards | • Over the last several years, the Air Force Space and Missile Systems Center has taken action aimed at preventing parts quality problems by issuing policy relating to specifications and standards. According to officials, it is requiring the GPS III program development contractor to meet these specifications and standards. |
| | • In February 2011, the Air Force's Space and Missile Systems Center, Missile Defense Agency, NASA, and the National Reconnaissance Office signed a memorandum of understanding (MOU) in February 2011 to encourage additional interagency cooperation in order to strengthen mission assurance practices. The MOU calls on the agencies to develop and share lessons learned and best practices to ensure mission success through a framework of collaborative mission assurance. Objectives include developing core mission assurance practices and tools; clear and executable mission assurance plans; a robust mission assurance infrastructure and guidelines for tailoring specifications and standards for parts, materials, and processes; and, establishing standard contractual language to ensure consistent specification of core standards and deliverables. |

Source: GAO analysis of DOD data and previous GAO reports.

[a]The Secretary of the Air Force and Chief of Staff of the Air Force issued the Air Force Acquisition Improvement Plan to recapture acquisition excellence by rebuilding an Air Force acquisition culture that delivers products and services as promised—on time, within budget, and in compliance with all laws, policies, and regulations. The plan consists of five initiatives: (1) revitalize the Air Force acquisition workforce, (2) improve the requirements generation process, (3) instill budget and financial discipline, (4) improve major Air Force systems source selections, and (5) establish clear lines of authority and accountability within acquisition organizations

[b]The ASD/NII's responsibilities included serving as the principal staff assistant on non-intelligence space matters; information technology, including National Security Systems; information resource management; and sensitive information integration. The ASD/NII also served as the principal staff assistant for issues such as command and control and net-centric capabilities.

[c]As part of this direction, the Deputy Secretary of Defense authorized the establishment of a jointly manned space office to restructure and replace the NSSO. The NSSO supported the Secretary of the Air Force who, as the DOD Executive Agent for Space, was responsible for developing, coordinating, and integrating plans and programs for space systems and the acquisition of DOD space major defense acquisition programs, and was responsible for executing the space major defense acquisition programs, when delegated that authority by the Under Secretary of Defense for Acquisition, Technology and Logistics. The specific roles and responsibilities of the DOD Executive Agent for Space are defined in Department of Defense Directive 5101.2, DOD Executive Agent for Space (June 3, 2003).

[d]GAO, Space Acquisitions: DOD Needs to Take More Action to Address Unrealistic Initial Cost Estimates of Space Systems, GAO-07-96 (Washington, D.C.: Nov. 17, 2006).

Congress and DOD have taken major steps toward reforming the defense acquisition system in ways that may increase the likelihood that weapon programs will succeed in meeting planned cost and schedule objectives.[12] In particular, DOD policy and legislative provisions place greater emphasis on front-end planning and establishing sound business cases for starting programs. For example, the provisions require programs to invest more time and resources to refine concepts through early systems engineering, strengthening cost estimating, developing technologies, building prototypes, holding early milestone reviews, and developing preliminary designs before starting system development.[13] These provisions are intended to enable programs to refine a weapon system concept and make cost, schedule, and performance trade-offs before significant commitments are made. In addition, DOD policy requires establishment of configuration steering boards that meet annually to review program requirements changes as well as to make recommendations on proposed descoping options that could reduce program costs or moderate requirements. Fundamentally, these provisions should help (1) programs replace risk with knowledge and (2) set up more executable programs.

While DOD has taken steps to implement the provisions, it is too soon to determine if Congress's and DOD's reform efforts will improve weapon program outcomes. For example, in June 2011 we reported on the Joint Requirements Oversight Council's (JROC) efforts to ensure trade-offs among cost, schedule, and performance objectives, as directed by the

---

[12] GAO, *Defense Acquisitions: Strong Leadership Is Key to Planning and Executing Stable Weapon Programs*, GAO-10-522 (Washington, D.C.: May 6, 2010).

[13] Weapon Systems Acquisition Reform Act of 2009 (WSARA), Pub. L. No. 111-23; DOD Instruction 5000.02, *Operation of the Defense Acquisition System* (2008).

Weapon Systems Acquisition Reform Act .[14] We found that the JROC did not always consider tradeoffs or influence tradeoff decisions, military services did not consistently provide high quality resource estimates to the JROC, and JROC did not consistently prioritize requirements and capability gaps. We recommended that the JROC establish a mechanism to review analysis of alternatives results earlier in the acquisition process, require higher quality resource estimates from requirements sponsors, prioritize requirements across proposed programs, and address potential redundancies during requirements reviews. The Joint Staff partially concurred with our recommendations and generally agreed with their intent, but differed with us on how to implement them.

## Remaining Challenges

The actions that the Office of the Secretary of Defense and the Air Force have been taking to address acquisition problems are good steps. But there are still significant barriers to ensuring investments are optimized, including fragmented leadership, the high cost of launch, uncertainty about the future for technology advancements, and disconnects between the fielding of satellites with user equipment and ground systems needed to take advantage of expensive new capabilities. In particular:

- Leadership. In past years, we have reported that a major challenge to leadership is that the community's authorities and responsibilities are spread across the department, and there is no single authority responsible for these programs below the President. Both the DOD and Air Force have taken a number of steps to streamline and clarify leadership for space. Time will tell whether these steps will help resolve issues such as a difficulty holding any one person or organization accountable for balancing needs against wants, for resolving conflicts among the many organizations involved with space, and for ensuring that resources are dedicated where they need to be dedicated. The department is still struggling with disconnects between programs that need to be linked together, such as a satellite program and its user equipment program. And at a higher level, we have reported that it still appears as if agencies involved in space

---

[14] GAO, *DOD Weapons Systems: Missed Trade-off Opportunities During Requirements Reviews,* GAO-11-502 (Washington, D.C.: June 16, 2011).

acquisitions do not coordinate to the extent that they can in such areas as launch acquisitions and space S&T planning. [15]

- Launch costs. A factor influencing how space programs are designed is the price of launch, which can range anywhere from around $100 million to well over $200 million. With prices being so high, programs often seek to maximize the "real estate" on board a satellite by including more capabilities than can sometimes be handled by a single program or within the time period desired for the program. Moreover, the Air Force recently developed a new launch acquisition strategy designed in part to contain launch prices, but given remaining knowledge gaps, achieving this outcome is uncertain. At the same time, potential new providers promise lower costs for launch, but none of them have been certified to launch the larger national security satellites, and it is uncertain whether their prices can stay low as they work to meet standards and expectations set by government agencies. The dilemma of high launch costs, in our view, makes it more important for the Air Force to gain insight into costs and pricing behind its new strategy and to have a complete understanding of the industrial base and related vulnerabilities as well as mission assurance activities and related costs. It would also behoove agencies to work together, not only to bring in new entrants which they are now doing, but in setting a future course for launch. S&T planning, for example, has been cited as a weak area for launch, even though investments in new propulsion and vehicle concepts have the potential to evolve capabilities and lower costs.
- S&T and related investments. Recent proposed funding cuts have raised questions about how future technology advancements will be achieved in space. The Space Test Program (STP) was targeted for termination in the fiscal year 2013 budget. STP was created in 1965 to serve as an integrator to provide launch opportunities for experimental satellites. This program enabled new technologies to get on orbit, and pave the way in an affordable manner for new space capabilities. STP has spawned many current and valuable space programs, most notably GPS. With the cancelation of this program, the Secretary of the Air Force has stated that the organizations that develop these new space technologies, including academic institutions, government laboratories, and others, will be required to shoulder the burden of launch costs, estimated at around $50 million

---

[15] GAO, 2012 Annual Report: Opportunities to Reduce Duplication, Overlap and Fragmentation, Achieve Savings, and Enhance Revenue, GAO-12-342SP (Washington, D.C.: Feb.28, 2012).

per year. DOD has also proposed cancellation of the Operationally Responsive Space (ORS) program. ORS was intended to provide short-term and low-cost tactical capabilities to warfighters. The ORS program's long-term goals were to reduce the cost of space development by fostering low cost launch methods as well as common design and interface methods. Average spending by the ORS program was about $100 million per year from fiscal years 2007-through 2011. While there are still investments available for the Air Force Research Laboratory and other organizations involved in S&T, as we mentioned earlier, planning for these investments has not been robust or very strategic. Another potential challenge to future space capability innovations is the Efficient Space Procurement (ESP) initiative, formerly known as the Evolutionary Acquisition for Space Efficiency (EASE). ESP is intended as a way to reduce costs for DOD space programs while improving acquisition outcomes by buying satellites in "block buys" instead of individually, accruing cost savings which are to be reinvested into a modernization program to evolve capabilities for future increments of that satellite program. At this time, it is unclear how this approach will ensure there will still be a focus on making significant leaps in technology or what the next generation of space systems will look like and be able to come into fruition.

- Disconnects between fielding satellites, ground systems, and user equipment. DOD faces challenges in synchronizing capabilities offered by new satellite programs with the ground control stations that are necessary for receiving and processing information from the new space systems, and in some cases, the user terminals that deliver this information to users.[16] When space, ground and user segments are not synchronized, there is the potential for wasted on-orbit capability and delays in the ability of users to take advantage of new systems. As long as this condition exists, the improvements being made to acquisition practices on the satellite side will be minimized. A few examples are highlighted below in table 3.

---

[16] GAO, *Defense Acquisitions: Challenges in Aligning Space System Components*, GAO-10-55 (Washington, D.C.: Oct 29, 2009).

**Table 3: Examples of significant disconnects between satellites, ground systems, and user equipment acquisitions**

| | |
|---|---|
| SBIRS | The first Space Based Infrared System (SBIRS) satellite was launched in May 2011 and carries scanning and staring sensors designed to provide early missile warning capabilities. However, DOD will not be able to fully utilize the data collected from the staring sensor because the ground segment software that is to process the sensor's data is not planned to be fully functional until at least 2018. This means that complete, usable data from the staring sensor will not be available until about 7 years after the satellite is on orbit. |
| GPS Ground System | Modernizations to the Global Positioning System (GPS) have also faced synchronization challenges between the GPS III satellites, which are currently under development, a concurrently developed new ground control system, and new military user equipment that will be able to utilize the capabilities of the new satellites. The new GPS ground control segment (OCX) is being developed to take advantage of the modernized capabilities of the GPS III satellites. OCX is required for full operation of the new GPS satellites, but the contractor does not plan to deliver the first increment of OCX until August 2015—15 months after the first planned GPS III satellite launch. Because of this disconnect, the GPS directorate is funding the development of a separate GPS launch and checkout system that is to provide an earlier command and control capability for the first GPS III satellite, but it unclear at this time when this capability will be delivered. This gap-filler capability will not enable the new capabilities offered by GPS III satellites, such as a jam resistant military signal and three new civil signals, so most of these capabilities will be unused until OCX Block 2 is delivered in 2016. |
| GPS User Equipment | DOD is planning to field new GPS user equipment on a variety of air-, ground-, and sea-based platforms to utilize the modernized military signal made available by the newer GPS satellites. Although the availability of the new signal on satellites would be operational within the next few years, user equipment is not expected to be fully fielded to the warfighters until many years later, possibly as late as 2025. As a result, the military services' ability to achieve a joint navigation capability, an essential element of conducting future military operations, as well as benefit from the jam-resistant and stronger new GPS signals may not be fully realized until a decade after the first GPS III launch. |
| FAB-T | The Air Force's Advanced Extremely High Frequency (AEHF) and the Family of Advanced Beyond Line-of-Sight Terminals (FAB-T) programs have experienced a problems with synchronization of various system components which will provide protected communications for nuclear and conventional forces as well as many airborne assets and ground command posts. As one of the primary user terminal programs associated with AEHF, FAB-T has experienced numerous problems and the delivery of terminals is not currently aligned with the AEHF satellite program. Specifically, current estimates show that FAB-T will reach its initial operational capability in 2017, 3 years after AEHF is scheduled to reach its initial operating capability. In the meantime, the Air Force plans to conduct an independent alternative with reduced requirements to mitigate risk. |
| Joint Space Operations Center Mission System | Another area where synchronization in system development may pose problems is the Air Force's Joint Space Operations Center Mission System (JMS) and Space Fence programs. JMS is to process data about space assets gathered by the Space Fence and other Space Situational Awareness (SSA) programs, and will increase DOD's ability to track objects in space from about 10,000 objects with the current system to over 100,000 objects. According to the Space Fence program office, JMS needs to be available when the Space Fence is fielded because the amount of data Space Fence will generate exceeds existing command and control system performance limits. JMS recently underwent a change to its acquisition strategy, dividing the program's development into two increments to reduce risk and more rapidly deliver needed capabilities. The first Space Fence radar site is scheduled to provide initial operational capability by the end of fiscal year 2017, and to avoid a synchronization problem, JMS needs to be operational by this time. |

Source: GAO analysis

## Concluding Remarks

After more than a decade of serious acquisition difficulties, DOD is starting to launch new generations of satellites that promise vast enhancements in capability. Moreover, given the nation's fiscal challenges, DOD's focus on streamlining leadership, fixing problems, and implementing reforms is promising. But there are still significant barriers to achieve acquisition success that need to be addressed to maintain space superiority in an era of fiscal austerity. All of the barriers—leadership fragmentation, launch costs, S&T planning, and disconnects between space and ground assets—require action from the Air Force and the Office of the Secretary of Defense as well as the participation and cooperation of all the military services, the intelligence community, and other agencies such as NASA and NOAA. Moreover, though successful launches are being experienced, problems within ongoing development efforts such as GPS III, indicate that space acquisitions are still at risk of significant cost and schedule problems, and attention to reforms must be sustained.

Chairman Nelson, Ranking Member Sessions, this completes my prepared statement. I would be happy to respond to any questions you and Members of the Subcommittee may have at this time.

## Contacts and Acknowledgments

For further information about this statement, please contact Cristina Chaplain at (202) 512-4841 or chaplainc@gao.gov. Contact points for our Offices of Congressional Relations and Public Affairs may be found on the last page of this statement. Individuals who made key contributions to this statement include Art Gallegos, Assistant Director; Maricela Cherveny; Laura Hook; Angela Pleasants; Roxanna Sun; Bob Swierczek; and Alyssa Weir.

# Related GAO Products

*2012 Annual Report: Opportunities to Reduce Duplication, Overlap and Fragmentation, Achieve Savings, and Enhance Revenue*, GAO-12-342SP (Washington, D.C.: February 28, 2012).

*Evolved Expendable Launch Vehicle: DOD Needs to Ensure New Acquisition Strategy Is Based on Sufficient Information*, GAO-11-641 (Washington, D.C.: September 15, 2011).

*Space Research: Content and Coordination of Space Science and Technology Strategy Need to Be More Robust*, GAO-11-722 (Washington, D.C.: July 19, 2011).

*Space and Missile Defense Acquisitions: Periodic Assessment Needed to Correct Parts Quality Problems in Major Programs*, GAO-11-404 (Washington, D.C.: June 24, 2011).

*DOD Weapons Systems: Missed Trade-off Opportunities During Requirements Reviews*, GAO-11-502 (Washington, D.C.: June 16, 2011).

*Space Acquisitions: DOD Delivering New Generations of Satellites, but Space System Acquisition Challenges Remain*, GAO-11-590T (Washington, D.C.: May 11, 2011).

*Defense Acquisitions: Challenges in Aligning Space System Components*, GAO-10-55 (Washington, D.C.: October 29, 2009).

*Global Positioning System: Challenges in Sustaining and Upgrading Capabilities Persist.* GAO-10-636. (Washington, D.C.: September 15, 2010).

*Polar-Orbiting Environmental Satellites: Agencies Must Act Quickly to Address Risks That Jeopardize the Continuity of Weather and Climate Data.* GAO-10-558. (Washington, D.C.: May 27, 2010).

*Defense Acquisitions: Strong Leadership Is Key to Planning and Executing Stable Weapon Programs*, GAO-10-522 (Washington, D.C.: May 6, 2010).

*Space Acquisitions: DOD Poised to Enhance Space Capabilities but, Persistent Challenges Remain in Developing Space Systems*, GAO-10-447T (Washington, D.C.: March 10, 2010).

*Space Acquisitions: Government and Industry Partners Face Substantial Challenges in Developing New DOD Space Systems.* GAO-09-648T. (Washington, D.C.: April 30, 2009).

*Space Acquisitions: Uncertainties in the Evolved Expendable Launch Vehicle Program Pose Management and Oversight Challenges.* GAO-08-1039. (Washington, D.C.: September 26, 2008).

*Defense Space Activities: National Security Space Strategy Needed to Guide Future DOD Space Efforts.* GAO-08-431R. (Washington, D.C.: March 27, 2008).

www.ingramcontent.com/pod-product-compliance
Lightning Source LLC
Chambersburg PA
CBHW080940290526
45795CB00007BA/2834